The Ultimate Guide to Ebook Publishing and Earning: A Step-by-Step Handbook for Success

Dr. Shambhavi Kumari

Published by Dr. Shambhavi Kumari, 2023.

THE ULTIMATE GUIDE TO EBOOK PUBLISHING AND EARNING: A STEP-BY-STEP HANDBOOK FOR SUCCESS

First edition. February 11, 2023.

ISBN: 979-8215007310

Written by Dr. Shambhavi Kumari.

Table of Contents

Preface

As a passionate writer and self-publisher, I understand the challenges and rewards of ebook publishing and earning. The digital era has opened up a world of opportunities for authors to share their work with a global audience, and earn a sustainable income from their writing. However, navigating the world of ebook publishing can be overwhelming, with a multitude of options and technicalities to consider. This book is intended to be a comprehensive and practical guide for aspiring authors and self-publishers, to help them navigate the process of ebook publishing and earning.

Through my own experiences, and insights from successful authors and publishers, I aim to provide readers with a step-by-step handbook for success in ebook publishing. This book will cover the entire ebook publishing journey, from understanding the different platforms available, to developing a marketing plan, to analyzing sales data and optimizing earnings.

My hope is that this book will empower readers to take control of their writing and earning journey, and inspire them to reach their full potential as successful ebook authors. Whether you are a seasoned writer or just starting out, I believe this book will be a valuable resource for your journey in the digital publishing world.

Happy reading and best of luck on your ebook publishing and earning journey!

The Ultimate Guide to Ebook Publishing and Earning: A Step-by-Step Handbook for Success

Introduction:

Ebook publishing and earning has become an increasingly popular means of sharing ideas, knowledge, and creativity with the world. With the rise of digital technology, it is now easier than ever to publish and distribute ebooks globally, reaching a wider audience and earning a profit from your work.

In this handbook, we will guide you through the process of publishing and earning from your ebook in simple, step-by-step instructions. From writing and editing your ebook to choosing the right distribution platform and marketing it effectively, this guide will provide you with all the information you need to succeed in the world of ebook publishing and earning.

Whether you are an aspiring author, blogger, or subject matter expert, this handbook will help you turn your passion into a successful and profitable venture. Whether your goal is to share your expertise, reach a new audience, or simply earn an extra income, this guide is the perfect resource for you.

So, let's get started and explore the exciting world of ebook publishing and earning!

Index

Chapter 1

1.0 Introduction to Ebook Publishing and Earning:

In the age of digital technology, ebook publishing has become a popular and lucrative way of sharing knowledge, ideas, and creativity with a global audience. The convenience of digital devices and the ease of access to the internet have made it easier than ever for individuals to publish and distribute ebooks, reaching a wider audience and earning a profit from their work.

For those who have a passion for writing or have expertise in a particular subject, ebook publishing provides a unique opportunity to turn that passion into a profitable venture. Whether you're an aspiring author, blogger, or subject matter expert, the potential to reach a wider audience and earn an income from your work is within reach.

In this chapter, we will explore the benefits of publishing an ebook and provide an overview of the ebook publishing and earning process. We will also discuss setting your goals for publishing and earning from your ebook, and help you understand the importance of having a clear objective in mind before you get started.

The world of ebook publishing and earning is full of opportunities and possibilities. Whether you are looking to share your expertise, reach a new audience, or simply earn an extra income, this guide will help you navigate the process and achieve your goals. So, let's get started and explore the exciting world of ebook publishing and earning!

1.1 Understanding the Benefits of Publishing an Ebook

Publishing an ebook can provide a range of benefits for authors, bloggers, and subject matter experts. By taking advantage of the global reach of the internet, ebook publishing offers the potential to reach a wider audience and build a reputation as an expert in your field.

★ **Wider audience reach:** One of the biggest benefits of publishing an ebook is the potential to reach a wider audience. With the ease of access to digital devices and the internet, your ebook can be downloaded and read by people all over the world.

★ **Increased visibility:** By publishing an ebook, you can increase your visibility and establish yourself as an expert in your field. This can lead to new opportunities, such as speaking engagements, consulting work, and even book deals with traditional publishers.

★ **Control over content:** When you publish an ebook, you have complete control over your content. You can choose what to include, how to present it, and how to promote it. This gives you the freedom to express yourself in the way that you see fit.

★ **Increased revenue:** Another benefit of publishing an ebook is the potential to earn money from your work. Whether you choose to sell your ebook through retail platforms, offer it for free with advertising, or monetize it through affiliate marketing, there are many different revenue models available to ebook publishers.

★ **Flexibility:** Ebook publishing offers a high degree of flexibility, allowing you to work from anywhere and at any time. You can write, publish, and promote your ebook from the comfort of your own home, or from anywhere in the world.

In conclusion, the benefits of publishing an ebook are numerous. Whether you're looking to reach a wider audience, establish yourself as an expert in your field, or earn an income from your work, the opportunities are there for those who take advantage of them. As we move forward, we will explore the ebook publishing and earning process in more detail, helping you to turn your passion into a successful and profitable venture.

1.2 Setting Your Goals for Publishing and Earning from Your Ebook

Before you embark on the journey of publishing and earning from your ebook, it is important to set clear and achievable goals. Having a clear understanding of what you want to achieve will help you to focus your efforts and make the most of your opportunities.

★ **Determine your target audience:** One of the first steps in setting your goals is to determine your target audience. Who do you want to reach with your ebook? What are their interests and needs? Knowing your target audience will help you to create content that appeals to them and to market your ebook in a way that reaches them effectively.

★ **Identify your niche:** To be successful in the world of ebook publishing, it is important to identify a niche for your ebook. Whether it is a particular subject or a unique perspective, having a clear niche will help you to stand out from the crowd and attract the attention of your target audience.

★ **Set revenue goals:** Another important goal to set is the revenue you want to earn from your ebook. Whether you are looking to supplement your income or create a full-time business, setting clear and achievable revenue goals will help you to focus your efforts and measure your success.

★ **Choose the right distribution platform:** The next step in setting your goals is to choose the right distribution platform for your ebook. There are many different platforms available, each with its own strengths and weaknesses. Consider factors such as the cost of distribution, the reach of the platform, and the ease of use when choosing the right platform for your ebook.

★ **Plan your marketing strategy:** Finally, it is important to plan a marketing strategy for your ebook. How will you promote your ebook and reach your target audience? Will you use social media, paid advertising, or a combination of both? Having a clear marketing strategy in place will help you to maximize your reach and increase your chances of success.

In conclusion, setting clear and achievable goals is a crucial step in the ebook publishing and earning process. By determining your target audience, identifying your niche, setting revenue goals, choosing the right distribution platform, and planning your marketing strategy, you can focus your efforts and maximize your opportunities for success. In the following chapters, we will explore these elements in more detail, helping you to turn your passion into a profitable venture.

1.3 An Overview of the Ebook Publishing and Earning Process

The process of publishing and earning from an ebook can seem overwhelming, but with the right steps and preparation, it can be a straightforward and rewarding experience. Here, we will provide an overview of the key steps involved in the ebook publishing and earning process.

★ **Idea Generation:** The first step in the process is to generate ideas for your ebook. Consider your areas of expertise, your passions, and the needs and interests of your target audience. The goal is to create a unique and engaging ebook that will appeal to your target audience.

★ **Content Creation:** Once you have your ideas, it is time to start creating your ebook. This may involve research, writing, editing, and formatting. The key is to create high-quality content that provides value to your target audience.

★ **Cover Design:** A professional cover design is crucial in attracting attention and generating interest in your ebook. Consider hiring a graphic designer or using a cover design tool to create a cover that stands out and reflects the content of your ebook.

★ **Distribution Platform Selection:** The next step is to choose a distribution platform for your ebook. Consider factors such as the cost of distribution, the reach of the platform, and the ease of use when choosing the right platform for your ebook.

★ **Pricing and Promotion:** Once your ebook is ready, it is time to determine the price and promote it. Consider the value of your ebook and the target audience when setting the price, and use your marketing strategy to reach your target audience and generate interest in your ebook.

★ **Monitoring and Optimization:** Finally, it is important to monitor your ebook's performance and make optimizations as needed. This may involve adjusting your pricing, improving your marketing strategy, or making changes to your ebook content.

In conclusion, the ebook publishing and earning process can be broken down into a series of straightforward steps. By generating ideas, creating high-quality content, choosing the right distribution platform, pricing and promoting your ebook, and monitoring and optimizing your performance, you can successfully publish and earn from your ebook. In the following chapters, we'll explore each step in more detail, helping you to turn your passion into a profitable venture.

Chapter 2

2.0 Writing and Editing Your Ebook

Writing and editing your ebook is an essential step in the publishing and earning process. This chapter will provide guidance on how to create engaging and high-quality content for your ebook, as well as tips for editing and refining your content to ensure that it meets the standards of your target audience.

★ **Research:** Before you begin writing, it is important to research your topic thoroughly. Gather information from reputable sources, take notes, and organize your thoughts. This will help you to write a comprehensive and accurate ebook that provides value to your target audience.

★ **Writing:** Once you have your research, it is time to start writing. Keep your target audience in mind and write in a style that is engaging and easy to understand. Consider using headings, subheadings, and bullet points to break up your content and make it more visually appealing.

★ **Formatting:** The way you format your ebook is important for readability and presentation. Consider using a clear and consistent font, spacing, and layout to make your ebook more attractive and easier to read.

★ **Editing:** Editing is a crucial step in the writing process. Review your ebook for grammar, spelling, and punctuation errors, and make any necessary corrections. Consider hiring an editor or proofreader to provide an objective critique of your ebook and help improve its overall quality.

★ **Refining:** After editing, it is important to refine your ebook to ensure that it meets the needs and expectations of your target audience. Consider getting feedback from friends, family, or beta readers, and make any necessary revisions to improve the content and readability of your ebook.

In conclusion, writing and editing your ebook requires a combination of research, writing, formatting, editing, and refining. By taking the time to create high-quality content that meets the needs and expectations of your target audience, you can ensure the success and profitability of your ebook. In the following sections, we will delve into further detail on each of these steps, helping you to turn your ideas into a well-crafted, engaging, and profitable ebook.

2.1 Getting Started: Brainstorming and Outlining Your Ebook

Getting started with the process of publishing and earning from your ebook can seem overwhelming, but with a clear plan and structure, you can make the process much more manageable. Now, we will focus on the initial steps of brainstorming and outlining your ebook, which will provide a foundation for your writing and editing process.

★ **Brainstorming:** Before you begin writing, it is important to brainstorm and get your ideas down on paper. Consider what topics or themes you want to cover in your ebook, who your target audience is, and what value you want to provide. Do not be afraid to get creative and experiment with different ideas until you find one that resonates with you.

★ **Outlining:** Once you have your ideas in place, it is time to start outlining your ebook. This will help you to organize your thoughts, establish a clear structure for your content, and ensure that your ebook is comprehensive and easy to follow. Consider using headings and subheadings to break up your content and make it more visually appealing.

★ **Key Points:** As you outline your ebook, make sure to identify the key points that you want to emphasize. This will help you to focus your writing and ensure that your ebook provides the value and information that your target audience is looking for.

★ **Research:** While you're outlining your ebook, it is also important to research your topic thoroughly. Gather information from reputable sources, take notes, and organize your thoughts. This will help you to write a comprehensive and accurate ebook that provides value to your target audience.

In conclusion, brainstorming and outlining your ebook is a crucial step in the publishing and earning process. By taking the time to plan and structure your content, you can ensure that your ebook is well-organized, comprehensive, and engaging.

2.2 Tips for Writing Engaging, Compelling Content

Once you have your ideas organized and outlined, it is time to start writing your ebook. To ensure that your content is engaging, compelling, and resonates with your target audience, it's important to put effort into crafting your writing. Here, we will provide tips and best practices for writing engaging, compelling content that your readers will love.

★ **Know Your Audience:** To write content that engages and resonates with your target audience, it is important to know who they are. Consider their interests, needs, and what value you can provide for them. This will help you to write content that speaks directly to their needs and keeps them engaged throughout your ebook.

★ **Write in a Clear, Concise Style:** Writing in a clear, concise style makes it easier for your readers to understand your content and stay engaged. Avoid using technical jargon or complex language that may confuse or alienate your readers. Instead, use simple, straightforward language that is easy to understand and follow.

★ **Tell a Story:** People are naturally drawn to stories, and incorporating storytelling elements into your ebook can help to engage and captivate your audience. Consider using real-life examples or personal anecdotes to illustrate your points and bring your content to life.

★ **Use Visual Aids:** Including images, charts, or other visual aids in your ebook can help to break up text-heavy sections and make your content more engaging. Consider using these tools to highlight key points, illustrate concepts, or add interest to your content.

★ **Write with Passion:** Writing with passion and enthusiasm for your topic will shine through in your content and help to keep your readers engaged. Consider your own experiences and insights, and use them to add depth and richness to your ebook.

★ **Edit and Revise:** Finally, it is important to edit and revise your content to ensure that it is well-written, free of errors, and engaging for your readers. Consider having a trusted friend or editor review your content for clarity, coherence, and overall impact.

In conclusion, writing engaging, compelling content is key to creating a successful ebook that resonates with your target audience. By following these tips and best practices, you can ensure that your content is well-written, easy to follow, and engaging for your readers. With a focus on clarity, storytelling, and visual aids, you can write an ebook that captivates your audience and provides value from start to finish.

2.3 The Importance of Editing and Proofreading Your Ebook

Once you have written your ebook, it is important to take the time to edit and proofread it thoroughly before publishing. This step is crucial in ensuring that your content is error-free, well-written, and professional, which can impact the overall success of your ebook. In this section, we will discuss the importance of editing and proofreading your ebook and provide tips for ensuring that your content is polished and ready for publication.

★ **Correcting Errors:** The primary purpose of editing and proofreading is to correct errors in your writing. This includes spelling, grammar, punctuation, and formatting errors that can detract from the overall quality of your content. By taking the time to carefully review your ebook, you can ensure that it is error-free and presents a professional image to your readers.

★ **Improving Clarity:** Editing and proofreading can also help to improve the clarity of your writing. This includes checking for awkward phrasing, confusing sentences, and ensuring that your ideas are presented in a logical and easy-to-follow manner. A good editor or proofreader can help you to identify areas that need improvement and make suggestions for how to clarify your writing.

★ **Enhancing Readability:** A well-written, error-free ebook will be more enjoyable and easier to read for your audience. By taking the time to edit and proofread your content, you can ensure that it is clear, concise, and free of distractions that can detract from the reader's experience.

★ **Building Trust:** Finally, a professional, well-written ebook can help to build trust with your audience. Readers are more likely to purchase and recommend ebooks that are well-written and error-free, and by taking the time to edit and proofread your content, you can demonstrate your commitment to quality and professionalism.

To ensure that your ebook is polished and ready for publication, consider using a professional editor or proofreader. These individuals can help you to identify and correct errors, improve clarity, and enhance the readability of your content. Alternatively, consider having a trusted friend or colleague review your ebook for errors and provide feedback on areas for improvement.

In conclusion, the process of editing and proofreading is an important step in the ebook publishing process. By taking the time to review and correct your content, you can ensure that your ebook is well-written, error-free, and professional, which can impact the overall success of your publication. With a focus on clarity, readability, and building trust with your audience, you can create an ebook that is well-received and valued by your readers.

2.4 Using Beta Readers to Get Feedback on Your Ebook

Beta readers are individuals who read your ebook before it is published and provide feedback on its content and style. This feedback can be invaluable in helping you to improve your ebook and make it the best it can be before it is released to the public. In this part, we will discuss the benefits of using beta readers, how to find beta readers, and how to use their feedback to make improvements to your ebook.

1. **Benefits of Using Beta Readers:** Beta readers can provide valuable feedback on your ebook, including constructive criticism and suggestions for improvement. They can offer a fresh perspective on your content, identify areas that need clarification, and help you to identify and correct errors before publication. This feedback can be especially helpful in identifying any potential issues with your content before it is too late to make changes.

2. **Finding Beta Readers:** Beta readers can be found through a variety of sources, including online communities, writing groups, and personal contacts. Consider reaching out to people who are familiar with your niche or writing style, and ask for their help in providing feedback on your ebook.

3. **Using Feedback to Improve Your Ebook:** Once you have received feedback from your beta readers, it is important to use it to make improvements to your ebook. This may involve making revisions to your content, correcting errors, or making changes to your style or tone. Consider each piece of feedback carefully, and use it to make the necessary improvements to your ebook.

4. **Balancing Feedback and Personal Vision:** While it is important to take feedback from beta readers into

consideration, it is equally important to balance this feedback with your personal vision for your ebook. Ultimately, it is your book and your vision, and you should be comfortable with the final product before publishing.

In conclusion, using beta readers to get feedback on your ebook can be a valuable step in the publishing process. By leveraging the expertise and perspectives of others, you can identify areas for improvement and make the necessary revisions to your ebook before it is released to the public. With the help of beta readers, you can ensure that your ebook is well-received and valued by your audience.

Chapter 3

3.0 Formatting and Designing Your Ebook

Formatting and designing your ebook is an important step in the publishing process. A well-formatted and designed ebook not only looks professional, but it is also easier to read and engage with. In this chapter, we will discuss the key elements of formatting and designing your ebook and provide tips for making it look its best.

★ **Choosing a Format:** There are several different formats for ebooks, including PDF, EPUB, and MOBI. Each format has its own advantages and disadvantages, so it is important to choose the format that best suits your needs. Consider factors such as compatibility with reading devices, ease of formatting, and ease of reading when making your decision.

★ **Designing the Cover:** The cover of your ebook is one of the most important aspects of its design. A compelling cover will attract readers and help to make your ebook stand out. Consider hiring a professional designer to create a cover that reflects the content and style of your ebook.

★ **Formatting the Text:** Once you have chosen a format for your ebook, it is important to format the text so that it is easy to read. Consider factors such as font size, line spacing, and margins when formatting your ebook. You may also want to consider including visual elements such as images or illustrations to enhance the reader's experience.

★ **Navigation and Table of Contents:** A well-designed table of contents and easy-to-use navigation can make your ebook easier to read and use. Consider using headings and subheadings to break up the content into sections, and include links to specific sections or chapters to help readers quickly find the information they need.

★ **Hyperlinks and Interactive Elements:** Including hyperlinks and interactive elements in your ebook can enhance the reader's experience and make it more engaging. Consider adding links to relevant websites or other resources, or including interactive elements such as quizzes or interactive maps.

★ **Quality Control:** Before publishing your ebook, it is important to review it carefully to ensure that it is well-formatted and free of errors. Consider having a second pair of eyes review your ebook, or use tools such as grammar and spell checkers to help identify any issues.

In conclusion, formatting and designing your ebook is a critical step in the publishing process. By choosing a format that is compatible with your needs and designing an attractive cover, formatting your text to be easy to read, and including hyperlinks and interactive elements, you can ensure that your ebook is professional, engaging, and well-received by your audience.

3.1 Choosing the Right Ebook Format for Your Content

When it comes to publishing an ebook, choosing the right format for your content is an important decision. The format you choose will impact not only the way your ebook is delivered to your readers, but also the way it is displayed on their reading devices. In this section, we will explore the most common ebook formats and help you choose the right one for your content.

★ **PDF:** PDF stands for Portable Document Format and is one of the most popular ebook formats. PDFs are ideal for ebooks that are text-based and designed to be read on a computer screen or printed out. PDFs are also easy to create, as most word processing software can export documents to this format.

★ **EPUB:** EPUB is an electronic publication format that is designed specifically for ebooks. EPUB files are optimized for reading on a wide range of devices, including tablets, smartphones, and e-readers. This format is ideal for ebooks that include images, graphics, or other multimedia elements.

★ **MOBI:** MOBI is an ebook format that is optimized for reading on Amazon's Kindle devices. If you plan to distribute your ebook primarily through Amazon, choosing MOBI as your format may be the best option.

★ **AZW3:** AZW3 is a format used by Amazon that is similar to MOBI, but it also supports multimedia elements such as images and videos. This format is ideal for ebooks that include rich media, but it is only supported by Amazon's Kindle devices.

★ **iBooks Author:** iBooks Author is a format used by Apple for creating interactive ebooks that can be read on the iPad and other Apple devices. If you plan to publish an ebook that includes interactive elements such as quizzes, multimedia, and other interactive elements, iBooks Author may be the right choice for you.

★ **PDF/X:** PDF/X is a format used for professional print production that is similar to PDF. This format is designed specifically for printing high-quality documents and is ideal for ebooks that will be printed.

When choosing a format for your ebook, consider the type of content you are publishing and the devices your readers will be using to access your ebook. If your ebook is text-based and will be read primarily on a computer screen, PDF may be the best choice. If your ebook includes multimedia elements and will be read on a range of devices, EPUB may be a better option. If you plan to distribute your ebook through Amazon, MOBI or AZW3 may be the best choice.

In conclusion, choosing the right ebook format for your content is an important decision. Consider the type of content you are publishing, the devices your readers will be using, and the distribution channels you plan to use when making your decision. By choosing the right format, you can ensure that your ebook is delivered in the best possible way and that your readers have the best possible experience.

3.2 Using Tools and Software to Design and Format Your Ebook

Designing and formatting your ebook can be a challenging task, but there are many tools and software available to help you get the job done. Here, we will explore some of the most popular tools and software for designing and formatting ebooks.

★ **Adobe InDesign:** Adobe InDesign is a professional-level design and layout software that is widely used by publishers and graphic designers. This software is ideal for designing ebooks that include complex layouts, images, and graphics.

★ **Microsoft Word:** Microsoft Word is a popular word processing software that can be used to create and format ebooks. While it may not have all the advanced features of InDesign, it is still a great option for ebooks that are text-based and have a simple layout.

★ **Calibre:** Calibre is a free and open-source software that can be used to manage your ebook library and convert ebooks from one format to another. This software is also a great option for formatting ebooks, as it includes features such as templates, styles, and the ability to convert to various ebook formats.

★ **Scrivener:** Scrivener is a writing software that is designed specifically for writers and can be used to create, format, and publish ebooks. This software includes features such as outlining, organization, and the ability to format ebooks for various devices and platforms.

★ **Vellum:** Vellum is a software designed specifically for formatting ebooks. This software allows you to create and format ebooks in a variety of formats, including EPUB, MOBI, and PDF. It also includes a range of design templates and features for creating professional-looking ebooks.

★ **Canva:** Canva is a graphic design software that can be used to create ebook covers and other design elements for your ebook. This software is easy to use and includes a range of templates and design elements that can be customized to meet your needs.

In conclusion, there are many tools and software available to help you design and format your ebook. Choose the one that best fits your needs, based on the type of ebook you are publishing, the complexity of your design, and your budget. With the right tools and software, you can create an ebook that is professional-looking and easy to read.

3.3 Tips for Creating a Professional-Looking Ebook Cover

Your ebook cover is the first thing readers will see when browsing for ebooks, and it can make all the difference when it comes to attracting potential buyers. A professional-looking cover can set your ebook apart from the competition and help it stand out in a crowded marketplace. Here are some tips to help you create a professional-looking ebook cover:

★ **Keep it simple:** A simple and clean design is often more eye-catching than a cluttered one. Use simple, legible fonts and a limited color palette to create a cover that is easy to read and memorable.

★ **Make it relevant:** Your ebook cover should be relevant to the content of your ebook. Consider using images or graphics that are related to the subject matter of your ebook to help entice potential buyers.

★ **Use high-quality images:** High-quality images and graphics are crucial to creating a professional-looking ebook cover. Make sure the images you use are clear, in focus, and of a high resolution.

★ **Choose the right font:** The font you choose for your ebook cover is important, as it should be easy to read and not overpower the cover design. Consider using a simple sans-serif font for the main title and a serif font for subheadings or additional text.

★ **Consider the size and aspect ratio:** Your ebook cover should be optimized for the size and aspect ratio of the device it will be viewed on, such as a tablet, e-reader, or computer. Ensure that your cover design will look good at different sizes and aspect ratios.

★ **Use software or hire a professional designer:** There are many software programs and tools available to help you design your ebook cover, such as Adobe Photoshop or Canva. Alternatively, you can hire a professional designer to create a cover that will stand out and make your ebook look professional.

In conclusion, your ebook cover is a crucial component of your ebook and can have a significant impact on its success. By following these tips, you can create a professional-looking cover that will help your ebook stand out and attract potential buyers.

3.4 Optimizing Your Ebook for Readability and Accessibility

In order for your ebook to be successful, it is important to make sure it is optimized for readability and accessibility. This means making sure the content is easy to read and accessible to as many people as possible, regardless of their reading level, language proficiency, or ability. Here are some tips for optimizing your ebook for readability and accessibility:

★ **Use simple language:** Your ebook should be written in simple, straightforward language that is easy to understand. Avoid using technical jargon or overly complex vocabulary, as this can be difficult for many readers to comprehend.

★ **Break up text with headings, subheadings, and bullet points:** Breaking up text with headings, subheadings, and bullet points can help make your ebook more readable and accessible. This makes it easier for readers to find the information they need and understand the content of your ebook.

★ **Adjust font size and type:** The font size and type you use for your ebook can have a significant impact on readability. Choose a font that is easy to read, and adjust the size accordingly so that it is not too small or too large.

★ **Include alternative text for images:** Including alternative text for images can help make your ebook more accessible for readers with visual impairments. Alternative text should provide a brief description of the image and its context in the ebook.

★ **Make use of hyperlinks:** Hyperlinks can help make your ebook more interactive and accessible. Use hyperlinks to link to other relevant resources, such as articles, videos, or websites, that can help enhance the reading experience for your readers.

★ **Consider translation:** If your ebook will be read by people in different countries, consider translating it into multiple languages. This can help make your ebook more accessible to a wider audience and increase its potential for earning.

In conclusion, optimizing your ebook for readability and accessibility is important for making sure your ebook is accessible and enjoyable to read for as many people as possible. By following these tips, you can make sure your ebook is easy to understand and accessible to a wide range of readers.

Chapter 4

4.0 Ebook Retailers and Distribution Platforms

Ebook retailers and distribution platforms have become essential for authors and publishers to reach a wide audience and monetize their work. These platforms provide a simple and efficient way for authors and publishers to sell their ebooks to readers around the world. Ebook retailers and distribution platforms are online marketplaces that sell digital books to readers. These platforms allow authors and publishers to upload their ebooks and reach a large and diverse audience without the need for physical bookstores. The most popular ebook retailers include Amazon Kindle, Apple iBooks, Barnes & Noble Nook, Kobo, and Google Play Books.

Ebook retailers and distribution platforms play a crucial role in the publishing industry by providing a convenient and cost-effective way for authors and publishers to reach a large and diverse audience. These platforms offer a wide range of benefits, including:

★ **Increased Visibility:** Ebook retailers and distribution platforms provide authors and publishers with a larger audience and increased visibility for their work. This increased visibility can lead to more sales and higher earnings for the author or publisher.

★ **Easy Access to a Global Market:** Ebook retailers and distribution platforms allow authors and publishers to reach a global market with ease. With just a few clicks, authors and publishers can make their work available to readers all over the world.

★ **Simple and Convenient Distribution:** Ebook retailers and distribution platforms simplify the distribution process by handling the sale, payment, and delivery of the ebook. This saves time and effort for the author or publisher and provides a seamless experience for the reader.

★ **Increased Control:** Ebook retailers and distribution platforms give authors and publishers greater control over the publication and distribution of their work. They can set the price, format, and availability of their ebook and make changes whenever they want.

★ **Analytics and Reporting:** Ebook retailers and distribution platforms provide authors and publishers with detailed analytics and reporting tools that help them understand their sales performance and make informed decisions about their publishing strategy.

In conclusion, ebook retailers and distribution platforms are essential for authors and publishers to reach a wide audience, increase their visibility, and monetize their work. With the right strategy and approach, authors and publishers can maximize their potential and achieve success through these platforms.

4.1 An overview of popular ebook retailers and distribution platforms

Once your ebook has been written, edited, and designed, it is time to publish and distribute it. There are many retailers and distribution platforms that you can use to publish and sell your ebook. Here is an overview of some of the most popular ebook retailers and distribution platforms:

★ **Amazon Kindle Direct Publishing (KDP):** Amazon's Kindle Direct Publishing (KDP) platform is one of the largest ebook retailers in the world. KDP allows you to publish your ebook directly on Amazon, where it can be sold to millions of Kindle users. With KDP, you can set your own price and earn up to 70% royalties on your ebook sales.

★ **Apple iBooks:** Apple's iBooks platform is another popular ebook retailer, allowing you to publish your ebook on the iBooks Store. iBooks offers a clean, user-friendly interface and allows you to reach a large audience of Apple users. iBooks also allows you to set your own price and earn royalties based on your ebook sales.

★ **Barnes & Noble Nook Press:** Barnes & Noble's Nook Press platform is another popular ebook retailer, allowing you to publish and sell your ebook on the Nook Store. Nook Press offers a variety of tools and resources to help you format, publish, and market your ebook. Like other retailers, Nook Press allows you to set your own price and earn royalties based on your ebook sales.

★ **Kobo Writing Life:** Kobo Writing Life is an ebook retailer and distribution platform that allows you to publish and sell your ebook on the Kobo Store. Kobo Writing Life offers a variety of resources and tools to help you format and publish your ebook, and also allows you to set your own price and earn royalties based on your ebook sales.

★ **Smashwords:** Smashwords is a distribution platform that allows you to publish and distribute your ebook to a variety of retailers, including Amazon, Apple, Barnes & Noble, and Kobo. With Smashwords, you can reach a large audience and earn royalties based on your ebook sales.

★ **Draft2Digital:** Draft2Digital is another distribution platform that allows you to publish and distribute your ebook to a variety of retailers, including Amazon, Apple, Barnes & Noble, and Kobo. Draft2Digital offers a variety of tools and resources to help you format, publish, and market your ebook, and also allows you to earn royalties based on your ebook sales.

When choosing a retailer or distribution platform, it's important to consider a variety of factors, including the size of the audience, the royalties you can earn, the tools and resources available, and the ease of use. By choosing the right retailer or distribution platform, you can reach a large audience, earn money from your ebook sales, and make your ebook a success.

In conclusion, there are many retailers and distribution platforms that you can use to publish and sell your ebook. By choosing the right retailer or distribution platform, you can reach a large audience, earn money from your ebook sales, and make your ebook a success. Whether you are a first-time author or a seasoned professional, there is a retailer or distribution platform that is right for you and your ebook.

4.2 Understanding the Pros and Cons of Each Platform

When choosing a retailer or distribution platform for your ebook, it is important to consider both the pros and cons of each option. Each platform has its own unique advantages and disadvantages, and it is important to understand these before making a decision.

★ Amazon Kindle Direct Publishing (KDP):

Pros: Amazon is the largest online retailer in the world and has a massive customer base, which means you have access to a large audience. The platform also provides easy-to-use tools for formatting and uploading your ebook, and allows you to set your own prices. Additionally, KDP offers royalty rates of up to 70% for books priced between $2.99 and $9.99.

Cons: Amazon has a strict review process and can reject your book for various reasons, such as poor quality or inappropriate content. They also have strict pricing guidelines, which can make it difficult to price your ebook competitively. Additionally, Amazon takes a significant portion of the revenue from each sale, meaning you may earn less from each book sold on their platform.

★ Apple iBooks:

Pros: Apple iBooks has a large customer base and provides a user-friendly platform for uploading and formatting your ebook. They also offer competitive royalty rates of up to 70%.

Cons: Apple iBooks is only available to users with Apple devices, meaning you may miss out on a significant portion of the ebook market. Additionally, Apple has strict formatting guidelines and a review process, which can be time-consuming and may result in rejection of your book.

★ Barnes & Noble Nook Press:

Pros: Barnes & Noble Nook Press is a well-established ebook retailer with a large customer base. They provide easy-to-use tools for formatting and uploading your ebook, and allow you to set your own prices. Additionally, they offer competitive royalty rates of up to 65%.

Cons: Barnes & Noble Nook Press is not as widely known as other ebook retailers, meaning your book may not receive as much visibility. Additionally, the platform has a smaller customer base compared to Amazon, which may limit the potential audience for your book.

★ Kobo Writing Life:

Pros: Kobo Writing Life offers a user-friendly interface for uploading and formatting your ebook, and allows you to set your own prices. The platform also provides a global distribution network, meaning you can reach readers in over 190 countries. They also offer competitive royalty rates of up to 80%.

Cons: Kobo Writing Life is not as well known as other ebook retailers, meaning your book may not receive as much visibility. Additionally, the platform has a smaller customer base compared to Amazon, which may limit the potential audience for your book.

★ Smashwords:

Pros: Smashwords offers a royalty rate of up to 85% for authors. Smashwords distributes ebooks to a wide range of retailers, including Barnes & Noble, Kobo, and Apple iBooks. Smashwords has a user-friendly interface, making it easy to upload and manage your ebook.

Cons: Smashwords has a smaller market compared to Amazon, meaning fewer potential readers for your ebook.

Smashwords may have limited visibility in certain countries. Smashwords has a smaller customer base compared to Amazon, which could affect the visibility and sales of your ebook.

★ Draft2Digital:

Pros: Draft2Digital has a wide distribution network that includes major online retailers such as Amazon, Kobo, and Barnes & Noble. Draft2Digital has a user-friendly platform that makes it easy for authors to publish and manage their ebooks. Draft2Digital offers higher royalty rates compared to other distributors, allowing authors to earn more from their ebooks.

Cons: Like Google Play Books, Draft2Digital sets the prices for ebooks, so authors have limited control over how their works are priced. Additional fees: Draft2Digital charges additional fees for some of its services, which may not be feasible for all authors. Draft2Digital does not offer as much marketing support as some other platforms, so authors may need to rely on their own marketing efforts to promote their ebooks.

Selling your ebook directly from your own website has the advantage of allowing you to build a direct relationship with your readers, and control the entire process from start to finish. However, this option may not be practical for everyone, and you will need to have a strong following and marketing plan in place to succeed. Ultimately, the best platform for you will depend on your goals, your audience, and your publishing experience. By taking the time to understand the pros and cons of each option, you can make an informed decision and choose the platform that is right for you.

4.3 Choosing the Right Platform for Your Ebook

With the increasing popularity of ebooks, it has become easier for aspiring authors to publish their works. With a multitude of ebook retailers and distribution platforms available, it can be challenging to choose the right one for your ebook. To make the best decision, it is important to consider a number of key factors, including your goals, audience, and publishing experience.

★ **Availability of Formatting Options:** Formatting is a crucial aspect of publishing an ebook. It determines how your book will look when it is downloaded and read. Some platforms provide extensive formatting options while others may limit you to a basic set of styles. Consider your needs and requirements before choosing a platform.

★ **Distribution Channels:** An ebook platform with a wide distribution network can help you reach a larger audience. Major players like Amazon Kindle Direct Publishing (KDP) and Barnes & Noble offer extensive distribution channels, making it easy for your ebook to be seen by millions of potential readers.

★ **Royalty Payments:** Different platforms offer varying royalty payment structures. Some offer a flat rate per ebook sold, while others may offer a percentage of the sale price. Consider which payment structure aligns with your financial goals before making a decision.

★ **Ease of Use:** Publishing an ebook can be a complex process, and you want to make sure that the platform you choose is easy to use. Look for a platform that has a user-friendly interface, clear guidelines, and helpful support.

★ **Cost:** While some ebook platforms are free to use, others may charge a fee for publishing and distribution. Consider your budget and the costs associated with each platform before making a decision.

★ **Marketing Support:** Marketing is an important aspect of publishing an ebook, and some platforms offer more support in this area than others. Consider whether you need assistance with marketing and choose a platform that provides the level of support you require.

You can publish your ebook on multiple publishing and retailing platforms. This is a common practice known as "wide distribution." By publishing your ebook on multiple platforms, you can reach a larger audience and increase your book's visibility. Keep in mind that some platforms may have exclusive distribution agreements, which means that you can only publish your ebook on their platform and not on others. Each platform has its own set of requirements and guidelines, so it's important to familiarize yourself with each before publishing your ebook. Be sure to read the terms and conditions of each platform carefully before making a decision.

In conclusion, choosing the right platform for your ebook requires careful consideration of your needs and goals. Take the time to research the various options available and select the platform that best meets your needs. Remember, the platform you choose can have a significant impact on the success of your ebook, so choose wisely. Ultimately, the right platform for your ebook will depend on your specific needs and goals. By taking the time to consider these factors and choose the platform that is right for you, you can increase your chances of success and maximize your earnings from your ebook.

4.4 Uploading and Publishing Your Ebook on Your Chosen Platform

Once you have completed writing, editing, formatting and designing your ebook, it is time to publish it on the chosen distribution platform. This can be an exciting moment, but it can also be nerve-wracking, especially if you are new to ebook publishing. Before you begin, it is important to make sure that your ebook is in the correct format and meets the requirements of your chosen platform. You should also double-check that your ebook is polished and ready for publication.

Once you are ready, follow these steps to upload and publish your ebook:

★ **Create an account on your chosen platform:** Before you can publish your ebook, you will need to create an account on the platform you have chosen. This will require you to provide personal information and set up a payment method.

★ **Prepare your ebook file:** Make sure that your ebook file is in the correct format and meets the requirements of your chosen platform. You may also need to create a cover image or cover page to accompany your ebook.

★ **Upload your ebook file:** On most platforms, you will have the option to upload your ebook file directly from your computer or other device. You may also need to provide information about your ebook, such as the title, author name, and description.

★ **Set your price and distribution options:** Most platforms allow you to set your own price for your ebook. You will also have the option to choose how widely your ebook will be distributed. For example, you may choose to make it available only on one platform or on several platforms.

★ **Preview your ebook:** Before you publish your ebook, you will have the opportunity to preview it and make any final changes.

★ **Publish your ebook:** When you are ready, you can hit the "publish" button to make your ebook available for purchase.

With these steps, you should be able to successfully upload and publish your ebook on your chosen platform. Remember, once your ebook is published, you can continue to promote it and reach a wider audience. Congratulations! You have successfully published your ebook.

Chapter 5

5.0 Marketing and Promoting Your Ebook

Now that your ebook is published and available for readers, it is time to start promoting it. Marketing and promoting your ebook is essential to reach a wider audience and increase sales. In this chapter, we will explore various marketing strategies that can help you reach and engage with potential readers.

★ **Utilize Social Media:** Social media is a powerful tool to promote your ebook and reach a large audience. You can use platforms such as Twitter, Facebook, and Instagram to share information about your ebook and engage with your followers. You can also join online communities and groups related to your niche and share information about your ebook with the members.

★ **Leverage Email Marketing:** Email marketing is a highly effective way to promote your ebook and reach a targeted audience. You can use your email list to send updates about your ebook, as well as offer exclusive discounts and promotions.

★ **Guest Blogging:** Writing guest posts on popular blogs and websites related to your niche can help you reach a new audience and promote your ebook. Make sure to include a link to your ebook in your author bio, and consider offering a discount or giveaway to encourage readers to purchase your ebook.

★ **Book Reviews:** Book reviews can be a valuable tool in promoting your ebook. Reach out to book bloggers and reviewers and offer them a copy of your ebook in exchange for a review. Make sure to include a link to your ebook in your email and provide them with any relevant information about your book.

★ **Book Giveaways:** Running a giveaway is a great way to generate buzz and promote your ebook. You can run a giveaway on social media, or through a website such as Goodreads. Make sure to follow the platform's rules and requirements for running a giveaway.

In conclusion, promoting your ebook is a crucial step in the ebook publishing and earning process. By utilizing various marketing strategies, you can reach a larger audience, increase visibility and ultimately, sales. Keep in mind that promoting your ebook takes time and effort, but with persistence and hard work, you can achieve your publishing and earning goals.

5.1 Understanding your target audience and their reading habits

Before embarking on the marketing and promotion of your ebook, it is essential to understand your target audience and their reading habits. This knowledge will enable you to effectively reach and engage with your potential readers, making your marketing and promotional efforts more efficient and impactful. By doing so, you will be able to reach and engage with your potential readers in a more meaningful and impactful way. By knowing who your readers are and what they look for in an ebook, you can make informed decisions about the content, format, and marketing of your ebook.

★ **Identifying your target audience:** This involves researching your potential readers and their demographics, interests, and reading habits. This information can be used to tailor your ebook to their needs and preferences.

★ **Understanding reading habits:** Different people have different reading habits, such as when and where they read, what devices they use, and what formats they prefer. By knowing your target audience's reading habits, you can optimize your ebook for their consumption.

★ **Researching the competition:** Knowing what other ebooks are available in your niche and how they are received by readers can help you understand what works and what doesn't in your market. This information can inform your own writing and marketing decisions.

★ **Using analytics to track reader engagement:** Many ebook retailers and distribution platforms offer analytics that can track reader engagement with your ebook. By monitoring this data, you can make informed decisions about how to improve your ebook and reach more readers.

In conclusion, understanding your target audience and their reading habits is a critical step in the ebook publishing and earning process. By taking the time to research your potential readers and track their engagement with your ebook, you can increase your chances of success.

5.2 Developing a marketing plan for your ebook

Once you have a good understanding of your target audience and their reading habits, the next step is to develop a marketing plan for your ebook. A marketing plan is a comprehensive strategy that outlines the steps you will take to reach and engage with your target audience and promote your ebook.

In order to effectively promote your ebook and reach your target audience, you will need to develop a marketing plan. Marketing your ebook involves creating a strategy for reaching and engaging your target audience, as well as promoting your ebook in various channels and platforms.

★ **Building your author platform:** This involves creating a presence for yourself as an author, such as a website, social media accounts, and a mailing list. Building your author platform can help you reach and engage your target audience and build your brand.

★ **Utilizing social media:** Social media is a powerful tool for promoting your ebook. By creating engaging content and using hashtags and keywords, you can reach potential readers and increase visibility for your ebook.

★ **Hosting book giveaways and promotions:** Hosting book giveaways and promotions can help you reach new readers and increase visibility for your ebook. You can use social media, mailing lists, and other channels to promote these events and reach your target audience.

★ **Partnering with bloggers and influencers:** Partnering with bloggers and influencers who are in your target audience can help you reach new readers and promote your ebook. You can collaborate on blog posts, social media campaigns, and other promotional activities to reach your target audience.

★ **Utilizing paid advertising:** Paid advertising, such as Google AdWords, Facebook Ads, and Amazon Advertising, can be a powerful tool for reaching new readers and promoting your ebook. By carefully targeting your ads to your target audience and monitoring their performance, you can maximize your results and reach more potential readers.

It is important to remember that marketing your ebook is a continuous process and requires ongoing effort and investment. To ensure the success of your marketing plan, it is essential to track your results and adjust your strategy as needed. This includes regularly monitoring metrics such as sales, engagement, and audience reach, and making data-driven decisions based on your findings.

In conclusion, developing a comprehensive marketing plan for your ebook is a critical step in promoting and selling your ebook. By setting clear goals, identifying effective marketing channels and tactics, and continuously monitoring and adjusting your strategy, you will be well on your way to achieving your publishing and earning goals.

5.3 Utilizing Social Media and Online Communities to Promote Your Ebook

In today's digital age, social media and online communities have become a valuable resource for promoting and marketing ebooks. With billions of people using these platforms daily, it is a fantastic opportunity for authors to reach a wide audience and promote their ebooks. In this part, we will explore how you can use social media and online communities to promote your ebook and increase its visibility.

5.3.1 Social Media Marketing

Social media marketing is a cost-effective way to reach a large audience and promote your ebook. The key to successful social media marketing is to understand your target audience and what platforms they are most active on. Some of the most popular social media platforms for promoting ebooks include Facebook, Twitter, Instagram, and LinkedIn.

Here are some tips for promoting your ebook through social media:

★ **Develop a strong online presence:** Start by creating a professional social media profile that represents you and your ebook. Use your profile to share information about your ebook, such as its title, cover, and a brief summary.

★ **Share engaging content:** Share content related to your ebook, such as sneak peeks, quotes, and behind-the-scenes insights. Keep your followers engaged by posting regularly and responding to their comments and questions.

★ **Utilize hashtags:** Hashtags make it easier for people to find your content on social media. Research the most popular hashtags related to your ebook's topic and include them in your posts.

★ **Collaborate with other authors:** Collaborating with other authors in your niche can help increase your reach and visibility. Share each other's ebooks, participate in online book clubs, and cross-promote on social media.

5.3.2 Online Communities

Online communities are another great way to promote your ebook. Many online communities cater to specific genres or interests, making them ideal for promoting ebooks to a targeted audience. Some popular online communities for promoting ebooks include Goodreads, Bookbub, and Reddit.

Here are some tips for promoting your ebook through online communities:

★ **Engage with your target audience:** Participate in discussions and engage with readers who are interested in your ebook's genre or topic. This is an excellent opportunity to build a relationship with your audience and promote your ebook.

★ **Share exclusive content:** Share exclusive content with members of online communities, such as sneak peeks, exclusive chapters, and behind-the-scenes insights. This will help build interest and anticipation for your ebook.

★ **Participate in book clubs:** Join book clubs related to your ebook's genre or topic, and participate in discussions. This is an excellent opportunity to connect with other readers and promote your ebook.

In conclusion, social media and online communities are powerful tools for promoting your ebook. By utilizing these platforms and engaging with your target audience, you can increase your ebook's visibility and reach a wide audience. So start building your online presence today and take advantage of these opportunities to promote your ebook!

5.4 Building Your Author Platform and Brand

As an ebook author, building your platform and brand is an important aspect of your success. Your author platform represents your unique voice and persona, and it helps you connect with your target audience and promote your ebook. In this section, we will cover the following key points to help you build your author platform and brand:

★ **Define your niche:** Identifying your area of expertise and target audience will help you tailor your content and marketing efforts to attract the right readers.

★ **Establish an online presence:** This includes setting up a website, creating social media accounts, and engaging with your audience through regular updates and interaction.

★ **Create content:** Whether it be blog posts, videos, or podcasts, creating valuable content for your target audience can help establish your expertise and build a following.

★ **Network with other authors and industry professionals:** Joining online communities and networking with other authors and industry professionals can help you gain exposure and make valuable connections.

★ **Consistency and authenticity:** Maintaining a consistent voice and being authentic in your interactions with your audience will help build trust and establish your brand.

★ **Utilize email marketing:** Building an email list and sending regular updates to your subscribers can help you reach a targeted audience and promote your ebook.

★ **Collaborate with others:** Working with other authors, bloggers, or influencers in your niche can help you reach new audiences and promote your ebook.

★ **Building a website or author blog:** Having a website or author blog is a great way to showcase your work, share updates, and connect with readers. You should consider using a user-friendly platform like WordPress to build your website.

★ **Building your brand:** Building your brand as an author involves creating a consistent image and messaging across all of your platforms. Consider your author bio, social media presence, website design, and author photo when building your brand.

★ **Continuously improving and growing your author platform:** Your author platform is not something that can be built overnight and must be consistently nurtured and improved. Continuously evaluate your platforms and strategies, and make changes as needed to better reach and connect with your target audience.

By following these key points, you can build a strong author platform and brand that will help you promote your ebook and reach your target audience. By developing a professional website, engaging on social media, and building an email list, you can effectively reach your target audience and promote your ebook. Investing time and effort in your author platform and brand will pay off in the long run as you establish yourself as an authoritative figure in your niche and grow your readership.

5.5 Offering Freebies, Discounts, and Special Promotions to Attract More Readers

In order to attract more readers to your ebook and increase sales, offering freebies, discounts, and special promotions can be a great strategy. Here are some key points to keep in mind when considering these tactics:

★ **Freebies:** Offering a free sample of your ebook, such as a chapter or two, can be an effective way to attract potential readers and give them a taste of your writing style and content. This can be especially useful for fiction writers, as readers are often more likely to buy a book if they have already read a portion of it and enjoyed it.

★ **Discounts:** Running a discount on your ebook for a limited time can also be an effective way to attract new readers. Make sure to promote the discount through your social media channels and email list, and consider offering a larger discount to your most loyal fans.

★ **Special Promotions:** Running a special promotion, such as a giveaway or competition, can also be a great way to attract new readers. For example, you could offer a free copy of your ebook to the first 50 people who buy it, or run a competition where the winner receives a free copy of your book.

When developing your marketing plan, it is important to carefully consider which promotions will be most effective for your specific audience and target market. With a clear strategy in place, you can leverage the power of freebies, discounts, and special promotions to achieve your goals for publishing and earning from your ebook. It is important to remember that these tactics should be used in moderation and not become a crutch for your marketing efforts. The quality of your ebook should be the main selling point, and these tactics should be used to complement and enhance your marketing efforts, not replace them.

Chapter 6

6.0 Earning from Your Ebook

Once you have successfully published and promoted your ebook, it is time to start earning from it. There are several ways to generate income from your ebook, including selling it on various retailers and distribution platforms, offering it for free as part of a larger marketing strategy, or using it to build your brand and attract more clients or customers to your business. Publishing an ebook can be a rewarding experience not just in terms of personal satisfaction but also financially.

★ **Selling your ebook:** One of the most straightforward methods of earning from your ebook is by selling it on various retailers and distribution platforms. This can include online bookstores such as Amazon Kindle Direct Publishing, Barnes & Noble Nook Press, or Kobo Writing Life. You can set your own price and receive a percentage of each sale.

★ **Offering freebies:** Offering your ebook for free can help you attract more readers and build your author platform. You can offer it as a free download in exchange for subscribers to your email list, or as a gift to your existing customers. This way, you can build your audience and collect valuable data about your readers, which can be used for future marketing efforts.

★ **Building your brand:** Another way to earn from your ebook is by using it to build your brand and attract more clients or customers to your business. For example, if you're a consultant, you can use your ebook as a way to showcase your expertise and attract new clients. You can also offer your ebook as a lead magnet to collect email addresses from potential clients, and then use that information to nurture those relationships and convert them into paying customers.

★ **Royalties and Licensing:** You can also earn royalties from licensing your ebook to others. For example, you can sell the rights to a publisher or offer it as part of a larger package deal to a corporate client. Additionally, you can also license your ebook to be included in a larger collection or bundle.

★ **Affiliate Marketing:** Finally, you can also earn from your ebook through affiliate marketing. This involves partnering with other businesses or individuals to promote your ebook in exchange for a commission on each sale. This can be a great way to reach new audiences and increase your earning potential.

In conclusion, there are many different ways to earn from your ebook, and the right strategy for you will depend on your goals and the type of ebook you have written. Whether you choose to sell it, offer it for free, use it to build your brand, or earn royalties and licensing fees, it's important to understand the different options available to you and choose the one that makes the most sense for your unique situation. In conclusion, earning from your ebook is a realistic and achievable goal. By understanding the different ways to earn, you can create a plan that works for you and maximizes your earning potential.

6.1 Understanding Different Revenue Models for Ebook Publishing

As an author, it is essential to understand the different revenue models available for publishing your ebook. This will help you make informed decisions about the best way to monetize your work and earn an income from your writing. In this chapter, we will discuss the most common revenue models for ebook publishing.

★ **One-time purchase:** In this model, the reader pays a fixed amount to purchase your ebook, and they have the right to access it indefinitely. This is the most straightforward revenue model, as it only requires a one-time payment from the reader.

★ **Subscription:** In this model, the reader pays a recurring fee, usually monthly or annually, to access your ebook. This model is often used by authors who publish serialized content, such as a series of short stories or a serialized novel.

★ **Freemium:** In this model, the reader can access a limited version of your ebook for free, but must pay to access the full version. This model is often used by authors who want to provide a sample of their work to potential readers, but want to earn income from those who are interested in the full content.

★ **Sponsorship:** In this model, the author is paid by a sponsor to produce and publish their ebook. The sponsor may be an individual, company, or organization, and the author may be required to include advertisements, product promotions, or other marketing materials within the ebook.

★ **Hybrid:** In this model, the author combines two or more of the above revenue models. For example, they may offer a limited version of their ebook for free, but require a subscription to access the full version. This allows the author to reach a wider audience, while still earning an income from those who are willing to pay.

Each of these revenue models has its advantages and disadvantages, and the best choice for you will depend on your goals, target audience, and the type of content you are publishing. By understanding the different options available, you can make an informed decision about how to monetize your ebook and earn an income from your writing.

6.2 Setting a Price for Your Ebook That Balances Value and Profitability

When it comes to publishing and earning from your ebook, setting the right price is a crucial decision. A price that is too high may discourage potential readers, while a price that is too low may not adequately compensate you for the time, effort, and resources you've invested in creating your ebook.

★ **The role of competition:** The prices of ebooks in your niche or market can help guide your own pricing strategy. It's important to understand what other authors and publishers are charging for ebooks that are similar to yours in terms of length, content, and quality.

★ **The value of your ebook:** What are the unique features and benefits of your ebook that set it apart from others in your market? These should be considered when determining the price of your ebook.

★ **The target audience:** The reader's demographic, interests, and spending habits should be taken into account when setting the price of your ebook. A general rule of thumb is to consider the amount of money your target audience is willing to pay for similar ebooks in your market.

★ **The cost of production:** From the time, effort, and resources invested in writing, editing, and formatting your ebook, to the costs of promotion and marketing, it is important to take these into account when setting the price of your ebook.

★ **Experimentation:** If you're not sure what price to set for your ebook, you can try different prices and monitor the sales and reviews to see what resonates with your audience.

Ultimately, the goal of setting a price for your ebook is to balance the value you are providing to your reader with the profitability you need to make your efforts worth your while. You may find that setting a slightly higher price for your ebook can increase its perceived value and attract more readers who are willing to pay a premium for quality content. Alternatively, you may choose to set a lower price to increase the volume of sales and make your ebook more accessible to a wider audience. When deciding on a price for your ebook, be sure to conduct market research and test different prices to find the one that works best for your ebook and your target audience.

6.3 Monetizing Your Ebook Through Advertising, Affiliate Marketing, and Other Methods

In the world of digital publishing, there are a multitude of ways to earn income from your ebook. Beyond simply selling copies, you can also monetize your ebook through advertising, affiliate marketing, and other methods. Here, we will explore these monetization methods in detail and help you determine which ones may be right for you and your ebook.

★ **Advertising:** One of the simplest ways to earn money from your ebook is to include advertising within the content. This could be in the form of banner ads or sponsored content that is relevant to your audience. This approach is particularly effective if your ebook has a large and engaged audience, as it provides an opportunity for businesses to reach potential customers through your platform.

You can include ads in your ebook, either as standalone pages or as sponsored content within your text. Some popular platforms like Amazon allow authors to monetize their ebooks through their Kindle Direct Publishing program, which allows them to include display ads on their ebook pages. You can also consider working with an advertising network such as Google AdSense, which matches you with advertisers and pays you for clicks on the ads placed in your ebook.

★ **Affiliate Marketing:** Another way to earn income from your ebook is through affiliate marketing. This is when you promote products or services related to the content of your ebook and receive a commission for any sales that are made through your unique affiliate link. To be effective, affiliate marketing requires careful selection of products or services that are relevant to your audience and align with your brand. This can be a great way to add value to your ebook by providing your readers with relevant products or services, while also earning a commission for your efforts. Some popular affiliate networks include Amazon Associates, Commission Junction, and Shareasale.

★ **Other Monetization Methods:** There are several other methods to monetize your ebook, including offering a paid membership to your author platform, selling merchandise related to your book, and offering exclusive content or access to your readers. You can also consider offering a premium version of your ebook, which includes additional content or features not found in the free version. You can offer speaking or coaching services based on the content of your ebook. The key to success with these methods is to understand your target audience and what they are looking for, so you can create offerings that meet their needs and desires.

In conclusion, monetizing your ebook through advertising, affiliate marketing, and other methods can help you turn your passion into a profitable venture. As with any business, it is important to be strategic and mindful of your audience and their needs in order to succeed. By exploring and implementing a variety of monetization methods, you can maximize your income and grow your brand as an author.

6.4 Analyzing Your Sales Data and Making Adjustments to Optimize Your Earnings

As an ebook publisher, it is important to regularly review your sales data and make necessary adjustments to optimize your earnings. The data you collect can provide valuable insights into your readers' preferences and behaviors, as well as your own performance as an author. In this chapter, we will discuss the importance of analyzing your sales data and the key metrics you should be tracking.

★ **Key Metrics to Track:** The first step in analyzing your sales data is to understand the key metrics you should be tracking. Some of the most important metrics include total number of ebook sales, Average sale price, Revenue generated from ebook sales, Conversion rate (the percentage of visitors to your website who make a purchase), Customer reviews and ratings, Popular keywords used to search for your ebook. The information regarding the number of ebook downloads and sales can be obtained from the platform or retailer where you have published your ebook. Additionally, you may want to keep track of the sources of your sales, such as social media or your author website, to see which marketing efforts are having the most impact.

Another important aspect to monitor is the average sales price of your ebook. If you find that your ebook is not selling as well as you had hoped, it may be necessary to adjust the price. On the other hand, if you are seeing strong sales, you may want to consider raising the price to maximize your earnings. In addition to sales data, it is important to monitor the feedback and reviews of your ebook. These can provide valuable insight into what readers enjoy about your book, as well as areas where you can improve.

★ **Analyzing Your Sales Data:** Once you have an understanding of the key metrics to track, you can begin analyzing your sales data. You can use tools like Google Analytics or your platform's reporting features to get a complete picture of your sales performance. Look for patterns in your data and use this information to make informed decisions about pricing, marketing strategies, and other areas of your ebook publishing and earning process.

★ **Making Adjustments to Optimize Earnings:** Once you have analyzed your sales data, it is time to make adjustments to optimize your earnings. This could include changes to your pricing strategy, marketing approach, or product offerings. For example, if you find that your conversion rate is low, you may want to consider offering a discount or free trial to encourage more visitors to make a purchase. Or, if you find that a particular keyword is driving a lot of traffic to your ebook, you may want to optimize your content and marketing materials to rank higher for that keyword.

★ **Continual Improvement:** Analyzing your sales data and making adjustments is an ongoing process. As your audience grows and evolves, so too should your approach to publishing and earning from your ebook. Continuously analyze your data and make changes to optimize your earnings, and you will be well on your way to becoming a successful ebook publisher.

In conclusion, analyzing your sales data is a critical step in optimizing your earnings as an ebook publisher. By tracking the right metrics and making informed decisions based on your data, you can continually improve your performance and reach your goals as a successful author.

Chapter 7

7.0 Conclusion and Next Steps

In this handbook, we have covered a wealth of information about the process of publishing and earning from your ebook. From understanding the benefits of this type of publishing, to writing and editing your content, to formatting and design, to retail and distribution, to marketing and promotion, to earnings and monetization, this guide has aimed to equip you with the knowledge and tools you need to be successful in the world of ebook publishing.

But the journey does not end here. The publishing and earning landscape is constantly evolving, and there is always more to learn and explore. As you continue on your own ebook publishing journey, consider the following next steps:

★ **Stay informed:** Keep up with the latest trends and developments in the ebook publishing industry by reading blogs, attending conferences and workshops, and networking with other authors and publishing professionals.

★ **Experiment with different methods:** Try new strategies for marketing and monetization to see what works best for you and your audience.

★ **Evaluate your progress:** Regularly review your sales data and adjust your pricing, marketing, and monetization strategies as needed to optimize your earnings.

★ **Build relationships:** Connect with other authors and publishing professionals to exchange ideas and build relationships that can help you grow and succeed in the industry.

★ **Write more ebooks:** The more ebooks you publish, the more opportunities you will have to reach a wider audience and increase your earnings.

With dedication, hard work, and a willingness to continually learn and grow, you can achieve great success in the world of ebook publishing.

7.1 Reflecting on Your Ebook Publishing and Earning Journey

Congratulations on successfully publishing and earning from your ebook! As you come to the end of this journey, it is important to take a moment to reflect on the process and what you have learned. This journey is unique to every author, and it's important to take the time to reflect on what you have learned and accomplished so far. Here are a few steps you can take to help you reflect on your experience:

★ **Review your goals:** Take a look back at the goals you set for yourself when you started this journey. How many of them did you achieve? What did you learn from the goals you did not achieve? First and foremost, take a moment to acknowledge your achievements. Whether you wrote a best-selling ebook, received positive feedback from readers, or earned a significant income from your efforts, these are all accomplishments that deserve recognition and celebration.

★ **Evaluate your marketing strategies:** Think about the marketing strategies you employed to promote your ebook. Which ones worked best for you? What could you have done differently to reach a wider audience? Next, consider what you would have done differently in hindsight. While we all make mistakes and missteps along the way, it is important to learn from them and use the experience to inform your future decisions.

★ **Assess your earnings:** Look at your sales data to see how much you earned from your ebook. What were the biggest factors that contributed to your success (or lack thereof)?

★ **Consider your readers:** Reflect on the feedback you received from your readers. What did they like about your ebook? What suggestions do they have for improvement?

★ **Analyze your publishing process:** Take a step back and evaluate the steps you took to publish and distribute your ebook. What was the most challenging part of the process? What could you have done better to make the process smoother?

By taking the time to reflect on your experience, you will be able to identify areas for improvement for your next ebook or for your future publishing endeavors. You can also use this time to celebrate your accomplishments and the growth you have experienced as a writer and publisher. Whether you are planning to continue publishing ebooks or not, the experience you've gained will be invaluable. Keep learning and growing, and most importantly, keep writing!

7.2 Celebrating your successes and learning from your challenges

After you've published and marketed your ebook, it's important to take a step back and reflect on your journey. Celebrating your successes and learning from any challenges you faced can help you grow as a writer and publisher, and set you up for even greater success in the future.

★ **Celebrate your successes:** One of the first things to do is to celebrate your successes. Whether you sold a few copies or a few thousand, each sale is a validation of your hard work and a recognition of the value you have brought to your readers. Take time to appreciate your achievements, and remember that every sale is a step closer to reaching your goals.

★ **Learn from challenges:** It is also important to learn from any challenges you faced along the way. Whether it was a slow start to your sales, a difficult time marketing your book, or a struggle to find the right distribution platform, there is always something to be learned from every experience. Take the time to reflect on what went well and what you could have done differently, and use this information to make improvements for your next project.

In conclusion, it is essential to celebrate your successes and learn from your challenges in the ebook publishing and earning process. By taking the time to reflect on your journey, you can continue to grow and develop as a writer and publisher, and set yourself up for even greater success in the future.

7.3 Planning for the Future and Continuing to Grow Your Ebook Business

After successfully publishing and earning from your ebook, it is important to look towards the future and think about how you can continue to grow and improve your ebook business. The following are some tips and strategies for doing just that.

★ **Monitor Your Sales Data:** Keep a close eye on your sales data and use it to make informed decisions about future projects. Look at which ebooks are selling well and consider writing more content in that niche. Also, take note of any trends or changes in sales and adjust your marketing strategies accordingly.

★ **Write More Ebooks:** Writing and publishing additional ebooks can help you reach a wider audience and increase your earnings. Consider writing ebooks on related topics, or exploring new niches that you are passionate about.

★ **Explore New Distribution Platforms:** As new platforms for ebook distribution become available, consider exploring them and adding your ebooks to their catalogues. This will give you a wider reach and allow you to tap into new audiences.

★ **Collaborate with Other Authors:** Collaborating with other authors can help you reach a wider audience and gain exposure for your ebooks. Consider co-writing an ebook or promoting each other's work.

★ **Stay Up-to-Date:** Keep yourself informed about the latest developments in the ebook industry, such as new technologies, distribution platforms, and marketing strategies. This will help you stay ahead of the curve and continue to grow your business.

★ **Never Stop Learning:** Continuously learning and improving is essential for success in any field, and the same is true for ebook publishing and earning. Consider attending workshops, conferences, or taking online courses to keep your skills and knowledge up-to-date.

By following these tips and strategies, you can ensure that your ebook business continues to grow and succeed in the future. With hard work and dedication, you can turn your passion for writing into a lucrative and fulfilling career.

7.4 Final Tips and Resources for Ebook Publishing and Earning Success

As you come to the end of this journey, it is important to take stock of what you have learned and to prepare for the future. Whether you have been publishing and earning from ebooks for a while or are just starting out, there are always new tips, resources, and tools that can help you grow your business. Here are some final pieces of advice to help you continue your success.

★ **Stay informed:** The world of ebook publishing and earning is constantly evolving. Stay informed by reading industry blogs, attending webinars, and networking with other authors.

★ **Be patient:** Success in ebook publishing and earning does not happen overnight. It takes time, effort, and persistence. Keep at it, and you will see your efforts pay off.

★ **Utilize technology:** There are a variety of software and tools available that can make your publishing and earning process easier. Experiment with different options to find what works best for you.

★ **Keep learning:** There is always more to learn about writing, editing, marketing, and monetizing ebooks.

Consider taking courses or attending workshops to expand your skillset.

★ **Seek feedback:** Continuously seek feedback from your readers and beta readers. This will help you identify what is working well and what needs improvement in your ebooks.

★ **Keep track of your progress:** Use tools such as analytics to track your sales, marketing efforts, and earnings. This will give you a clear picture of your success and help you make informed decisions about your future.

★ **Stay organized:** Create a system for keeping track of your ebooks, sales, and marketing efforts. This will help you stay on top of your business and make it easier to track your progress.

In conclusion, ebook publishing and earning is a challenging and rewarding journey. By following the tips and resources outlined in this book, you will be well on your way to creating ebooks that people want to read and earn from them. Good luck!

Sample Book Proposal

A sample book proposal based on the content of "The Ultimate Guide to Ebook Publishing and Earning: A Step-by-Step Handbook for Success"

Title: The Ultimate Guide to Ebook Publishing and Earning: A Step-by-Step Handbook for Success

Overview: This book is a comprehensive guide to the process of publishing and earning from ebooks. It is a step-by-step handbook that is designed to help authors understand the intricacies of the ebook publishing world and monetize their work.

The book provides a thorough understanding of the ebook retailing and distribution platforms and how to choose the right platform that aligns with your goals. It also covers the crucial aspect of understanding your target audience and their reading habits and developing a marketing plan to promote your ebook.

In addition to this, the book also covers building your author platform and brand, offering freebies, discounts, and special promotions to attract more readers, and setting a price for your ebook that balances value and profitability.

The author also sheds light on the various methods to monetize your ebook through advertising, affiliate marketing, and other techniques, as well as analyzing your sales data to optimize your earnings.

This book aims to provide a holistic approach to ebook publishing and earning that benefits both novice and experienced authors. It is a valuable resource that is perfect for anyone looking to monetize their writing and make a living as a self-published author.

Target audience: The book is aimed at anyone looking to publish an ebook and earn money from it, be it novice or experienced authors. It caters to writers who want to self-publish their work and establish their brand, as well as those who want to increase their ebook earnings.

Marketing plan: The author intends to market the book through various channels, including social media platforms like Twitter, LinkedIn, and Facebook. The author will also leverage her professional network and use book promotion websites and book reviews to generate awareness and interest in the book.

The author plans to offer the book at a competitive price that will attract potential readers and is in line with other similar books in the market. Additionally, the author will offer discounts and promotions to entice readers to purchase the book.

Competitive analysis: There are several books on ebook publishing and earning, but this book stands out due to its comprehensive approach to the subject matter. The book is written in an easy-to-understand language and is suitable for both novice and experienced authors. It is a valuable resource for anyone looking to make a career out of self-publishing.

Conclusion: This book is a must-read for anyone interested in publishing and earning from ebooks. It provides an in-depth understanding of the ebook publishing world and the tools needed to make a living as a self-published author. With its comprehensive approach and easy-to-understand language, this book is a valuable resource that will help readers achieve success in the ebook publishing world.

Sample Book Outline

A sample book outline based on the content of "The Ultimate Guide to Ebook Publishing and Earning: A Step-by-Step Handbook for Success":

I. Introduction

- Explanation of the importance of ebook publishing in today's world
- Brief overview of what the book will cover

II. Preparing to Publish Your Ebook

- Chapter on choosing the right topic and genre
- Chapter on writing and editing your ebook
- Chapter on designing your ebook cover

III. Choosing and Uploading Your Ebook to a Platform

- Chapter on understanding the pros and cons of each platform
- Chapter on choosing the right platform for your ebook
- Chapter on uploading and publishing your ebook on your chosen platform

IV. Promoting Your Ebook

- Chapter on understanding your target audience and their reading habits

- Chapter on developing a marketing plan for your ebook
- Chapter on utilizing social media and online communities to promote your ebook
- Chapter on building your author platform and brand
- Chapter on offering freebies, discounts, and special promotions to attract more readers

V. Monetizing Your Ebook

- Chapter on setting a price for your ebook that balances value and profitability
- Chapter on earning from your ebook
- Chapter on monetizing your ebook through advertising, affiliate marketing, and other methods
- Chapter on analyzing your sales data and making adjustments to optimize your earnings

VI. Conclusion

- Reflection on your ebook publishing and earning journey
- Final thoughts and encouragement

VII. End Matter

- Appendix (e.g. resources for further reading)
- Glossary of terms
- About the author
- Index

Note: This is just a sample book outline and can be customized and expanded upon based on the author's preferences and needs.

Sample Ebook Formatting Checklist

A sample Ebook Formatting Checklist that can be used as a reference for formatting an ebook:

1. **Cover Design:** Ensure the cover image is high quality and professional-looking, with a design that is relevant to the content and genre of the book.

2. **Table of Contents:** Create an easily navigable table of contents with clickable links for each chapter/section.

3. **Font and Layout:** Choose a clear, legible font and make sure it is consistent throughout the book. Ensure the layout is clean and easy to read.

4. **Images and Graphics:** Check that all images and graphics are high quality and optimized for digital viewing.

5. **Paragraph Formatting:** Use proper indentation and line spacing to make the text easily readable.

6. **Headers and Footers:** Add headers and/or footers that include the book title, author name, and page numbers.

7. **Copyright Page:** Include a copyright page with all necessary information, including the book title, author name, copyright date, and any relevant disclaimers.

8. **Formatting for Different Devices:** Test the ebook on different devices (e.g. Kindle, iPad, phone) to ensure it displays properly and is easily readable.

9. **Links and References:** Check that all links and references work properly and are up-to-date.

10. **Metadata:** Optimize the book's metadata for search engines and online retailers, including title, author name, description, and relevant keywords.

Keep in mind that this is just a sample checklist and the specific formatting requirements may vary based on the chosen publishing platform and ebook format.

Sample Ebook Promotion Checklist

A sample Ebook Promotion Checklist:
Before Launch:

- Identify your target audience and their reading habits
- Develop a marketing plan for your ebook
- Build your author platform and brand
- Set a price for your ebook that balances value and profitability
- Monetize your ebook through advertising, affiliate marketing, and other methods
- Analyze your sales data and make adjustments to optimize your earnings

During Launch:

- Use social media and online communities to promote your ebook
- Offer freebies, discounts, and special promotions to attract more readers
- Utilize paid advertising to increase visibility
- Reach out to book bloggers and reviewers for reviews and features
- Create a launch event or virtual book tour to generate buzz
- Send out press releases to relevant media outlets

Post Launch:

- Continue to promote your ebook on social media and through targeted advertising
- Consider running a limited-time sale or promotion to drive additional sales
- Utilize email marketing to stay in touch with readers and announce new releases
- Offer free samples or previews to entice new readers
- Respond to reviews and engage with readers on social media
- Analyze sales data to identify trends and adjust your marketing strategy as needed.

By using this Ebook Promotion Checklist, you can ensure that you are doing everything possible to promote and market your ebook effectively, maximizing its visibility, and driving sales.

Glossary of Terms

A list of terms and definitions related to ebook publishing and earning:

1. **Ebook:** A digital book that can be read on electronic devices such as e-readers, tablets, and smartphones.
2. **E-publishing:** The process of publishing digital content, including ebooks.
3. **Formatting:** The process of designing the layout and appearance of an ebook.
4. **DRM (Digital Rights Management):** A technology used to restrict the unauthorized use or sharing of digital content, including ebooks.
5. **Metadata:** Information about an ebook, such as the title, author, and description, that helps readers discover and identify the book.
6. **ISBN (International Standard Book Number):** A unique identifier assigned to each edition and variation of a book.
7. **Conversion:** The process of transforming a manuscript or other format into an ebook.
8. **Royalties:** The percentage of sales earned by the author or publisher for each copy of the ebook sold.
9. **Distribution:** The process of making an ebook available for purchase and download through online retailers and other channels.
10. **Marketing:** The activities and strategies used to promote an

ebook and increase its visibility and sales.

11. **Affiliate marketing:** A marketing strategy in which affiliates promote an ebook and earn a commission for each sale made through their unique referral link.

12. **Promotions:** Special offers, discounts, and other incentives used to attract readers and increase sales of an ebook.

13. **Sales data:** Information about the number of copies of an ebook sold, as well as other metrics such as revenue and conversion rates.

14. **Keywords:** Words or phrases used to optimize an ebook's discoverability and search engine rankings.

15. **Branding:** The process of establishing a unique identity and reputation for an author or ebook.

Don't miss out!

Visit the website below and you can sign up to receive emails whenever Dr. Shambhavi Kumari publishes a new book. There's no charge and no obligation.

https://books2read.com/r/B-A-WSWW-KZLFC

BOOKS2READ

Connecting independent readers to independent writers.

About the Author

Dr. Shambhavi Kumari is an accomplished teacher educator with over 14 years of experience in teaching at the B.Ed. and M.Ed. levels in various colleges and universities. As the current principal of a B.Ed. college, Dr. Kumari is responsible for the overall management and development of the institution.

Dr. Kumari holds a Ph.D in Education from Banaras Hindu University (BHU), Varanasi, and has also qualified for the NET-JRF in Education conducted by UGC. She has a diverse educational background, holding degrees in M.A. with English literature, B.Ed, M.Ed., and M.Phil (Education).

Dr. Kumari has a strong publication record, with extensive work on the topics of Teacher Education, Education for Scheduled Tribes, Language teaching, and ICT. She has also been actively involved in seminars and workshops for teachers, making significant contributions to the field of education. With her keen interest in ICT and its application in Education, Dr. Kumari has been able to integrate technology in the teaching-learning process and make it more effective.